BEDROOMS

STYLISH IDEAS

BEDROOMS

A collection edited by: Soledad Lorenzo

LeadingInternationalKeyServices

Barcelona, Spain

Author: Soledad Lorenzo
Work conception: Carles Broto
Publisher: Arian Mostaedi

Production & Graphic design: Francisco Orduña
English texts: Gina Cariño
Compilation, photo material & text information: American Book Services (USA)

© Carles Broto i Comerma
Ausias Marc 20, 4
08010 BARCELONA
Tel.: 34-3-301 21 99   Fax: 34-3-302 67 97
e-mail:links@xarop.com

ISBN: 84-89861-29-3
D. L.: 38188/99

Printed in Spain

contents

introduction

Slumberland, the paradise of dreams, exists. It is a part of the home, and every day, sooner or later, we retire to it. A refuge from the challenges of life, the bedroom is where we feel safe from everything, where our tired bodies may rest beneath a mantle of sheets and we can sink our heads into a pillow. In this position our minds make a quick recapitulation of the day's events and formulate plans for tomorrow, prompting both tears and smiles. In its extreme intimacy, the bedroom is also the best place in which to conceive life. Many, too, end life here.

Everything in the bedroom is familiar and relaxing, and this friendly atmosphere embraces us, as on a warm lap or in a mother's womb, so that at the end of the day we feel protected, almost the way we once were. There is something therapeutic about this puerile or even atavistic feeling after hours on end of furious activity, when our bodies surrender at long last to a well-deserved, albeit temporary, lethargy.

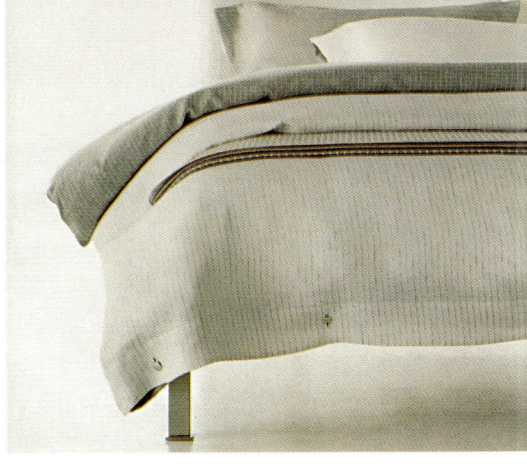

Materializing this private space of repose is, without a doubt, a transcendental task requiring creativity. The by now hackneyed feng-shui fashion warns of the danger of filling this room with television sets, computers, telephones and the like, objects which assault our rest, in the same way that our grandmothers advised us to avoid plants and flowers, which, greedy for oxygen, would suck in all the air for themselves at night, like bloodsucking vampires.

When defining the atmosphere that is to embrace our still, sleeping bodies, it is best to aim for an uncluttered, quiet space. Just the right temperature, neither too low nor too high, will help us fall into the arms of Morpheus. A cautious and sensitive use of colors and textures will play on our senses and lull us, ever so gently, into a sweet and silent slumberland. Serene order in the arrangement of furniture and an intelligent manipulation of light will then help us wake up in a place we have made our own, a place we feel good in. After all, don't we spend a third of our lifetime asleep?

Hence, whatever its size, the bedroom must be an oasis of peace. On the whole, this book presents spaces which are small and unpretentious yet functionally eloquent and decorated with a subtle touch of sensuality: beds coated with soft fabrics in winter, textures that brush against the skin in a way that intensifies the pleasure of idleness on a non-working day, gauzy textiles that freshen up the room in summer, furniture specially chosen to shape the space, and delicate plays of color that dissolve together to brighten and cheer up the room.

A wide range of images serves as a guiding thread, endeavoring to nourish our eyes with suggestions that are in tune with our personal way of creating the home. We hope that the readers will enjoy the book, and that each will be encouraged to invent their own private chamber of dreams.

Soledad Lorenzo

sweet

dreams

The bedroom is the resting place, a space that welcomes, envelopes, calms. It is the night room, a peaceful place in which our bodies can succumb to a healthy and well-deserved lethargy. These pages show some decorative tricks that help to make it more conducive to a deep and blissful repose.

a place to rest
new decorative concepts for the bedroom

The bedroom as a place in which to relax: this concept has replaced the traditional idea of the bedroom as a mere depository for sleeping bodies. The room once thought of mainly as a space in which to put the bed has become a place for relaxing, studying or even working. A good mix of the elements comprising such a multipurpose environment is the key to achieving a harmonious, pleasant, cosy and especially personal bedroom.

The quartet that forms the traditional bedroom set – the bed itself, the bedside tables, the chest of drawers and the closet – remains valid, but we are free to organize the bedroom as we please, depending on our needs, our tastes and the actual space available. For many, the bedroom is the closest thing to the room of one's own Virginia Woolf deemed indispensable. One may go for a minimalist design and strip it of everything one does not consider absolutely indispensable, or create a more cluttered environment, a sort of house within a house.

From the new tendencies that point toward pure of spaces combined with an eastern touch – such as a certain way of manipulating daylight and claddings, with feng-shui as

the maximum metaphysical-spiritual criterion – to reinterpretations of classical ideas, the planning of the bedroom emerges as an at once necessary and fascinating task.

The preceding page shows a magnificent case of two opposed solutions. In the upper left margin is an example of the house within a house, where an intimate, private sleeping zone is expressed as a continuation of a more social, public sphere. The color of the couches and low table strikes a contrast with the bright surrounding atmosphere, resulting in a chromatic differentiation of uses. Light is what gives the room its sense of unity, with the windows giving rhythm and verticality to the horizontal continuum formed by the sofas, the table and the bed.

The bedroom shown on the right is a mix of eastern and western conceptions. The bed is supported by short wooden legs, and framed beneath by a mat whose pattern stands out in the overall whiteness.

The room's chromatic uniformity is only broken by a rocking chair with a wooden structure and animal motifs for upholstery, and by three vertically aligned paintings in the gap between two windows. The atmosphere is nice and bright, stripped and bathed in daylight: the perfect setting for an object that competes in importance with the actual bed. This wrought iron sculpture of organic shapes is a strong counterpoint to the pure geometry of the room.

Above, a consolation for romantics: the 'put your own style' style of the nineties. Headboard and sidetable with gray details, a chessboard floor, and a large frameless mirror on the floor, simply leaning against the wall. No decorative elements other than the sheer richness of materials and the pureness of the white that invades the space altogether.

The number of decorative elements in a bedroom need not be proportional to its dimensions. Shown here is a large space where austerity is brought to an extreme, with pure forms and the absence of anything that is not absolutely indispensable. The bed is the axis around which the entire room revolves. Since it is the only piece of furniture, its personality is strongly defined: pure lines, natural materials, and functionality above all. Note its strong geometric character, not only in design but also in the way it relates to the space that contains it. The large wooden headboard stretches on to one side to serve as a support for a night table, a simple board of the same material.

The rhythm of the room is marked by the sequence of beams overhead, as well as by the play of perpendiculars between ceiling, floor and walls. The bed reflects the room, reproducing the tension of its perpendicular lines in the interaction between the headboard, the night table and the base of the bed, which is also of wood. A white lamp clamped to the edge of the night table provides illumination. It is a highly versatile model, with articulations enabling it to take on different positions. The lamp can be made to focus on the bed, or adjusted to shine on it indirectly. On the other side of the bed, close to the wall, a cylindrical lamp illuminates the transition between interior and exterior.

Though suggestive, this is a risky design to propose. In the end it is the user of the bedroom whose task it is to give sense and sensibility to the space. The absence of decor is intentional, very much in keeping with the eastern-inspired line mentioned above. Europe discovered and assimilated oriental styles long ago, but its fascination with the Far East then involved the richness of fabrics and materials, or the overall exuberance of Asian cultures, particularly Chinese. Asia's lacquered objects, silks and color combinations captivated European artists and designers of the early 1900s and were influential in the shaping of the style known as Modernisme, Art Nouveau or Liberty. Only in the past thirty years have we looked farther, towards Japan and its Zen influences. Thanks to this new way of looking east, ideas like void, harmony, serenity, movement, content and chromatic frugality form the basis of a new style whereby, more than ever, less is more.

If there is at all a rule that defines the latest trends in bedroom decoration, it has got to be this: anything goes. Nevertheless, there is a constant: the importance of materials. In all six proposals illustrated on this page, materials play a leading role.

Let us begin with the top right and move clockwise. The first two bedrooms draw attention to a dominant use of wood and cloth. The top headboard, padded and covered with textile, is of the curtain type, hanging from a wooden bar at both far ends. The second headboard rests on the whole length of the horizontal bar of a structure, and is a fine sheet of wood that bends like cardboard. Although we can find many similarities between the two proposals, they are radically opposed in geometry: the straight line governs the former, the curve dominates the latter. The third bedroom shows a reinterpretation of the traditional metal-framed bed, whose austere, even clinical look contrasts with the cylindrical, almost polka-dot-patterned jar.

The bottom left picture is proof that white need not be synonymous with cold. A wooden bed and a matching night table combine classicism and chromatic depuration. Our attention is drawn to the floorboards, which give the space a sense of warmth, and to the large window, through which daylight shines in. Wood and textile are dominant again in the last two cases. The middle left picture shows how the bedroom and sitting room functions can be brought together in a single space. The bed is framed by a huge wooden panel that serves as a support for the actual headboard, upholstered in green velvet, as well as for the night tables. To one side is the sitting room space, where a wooden structure forms both a sofa and a side table.

The top left picture shows a balanced combination of materials. Textile and metal come together in an almost minimalist composition. The folding night table is the perfect solution for a bedroom stripped of all elements that are not strictly functional.

a very personal atmosphere

The bedroom is the most private part of the house. In a place reserved for ourselves, we are free to defy criteria that tend to be sacred in other areas of the house, such as functionality in the kitchen, breadth for the living room and order in the study or office. In the bedroom we dictate our own rules, making it an extension of ourselves. One can use it as a testing ground, for example, where neither dimensions nor budgets are determining factors. It's all a matter of detail. Something as seemingly trivial as the knob of a closet can become the room's main decorative element. The same can be said for bedcovers. Light colors without patterns help to make a room look larger, but this is not necessarily the only criterion to work around. Below right, a discreet bow ties the cover to the leg of the bed, tapering its profile.

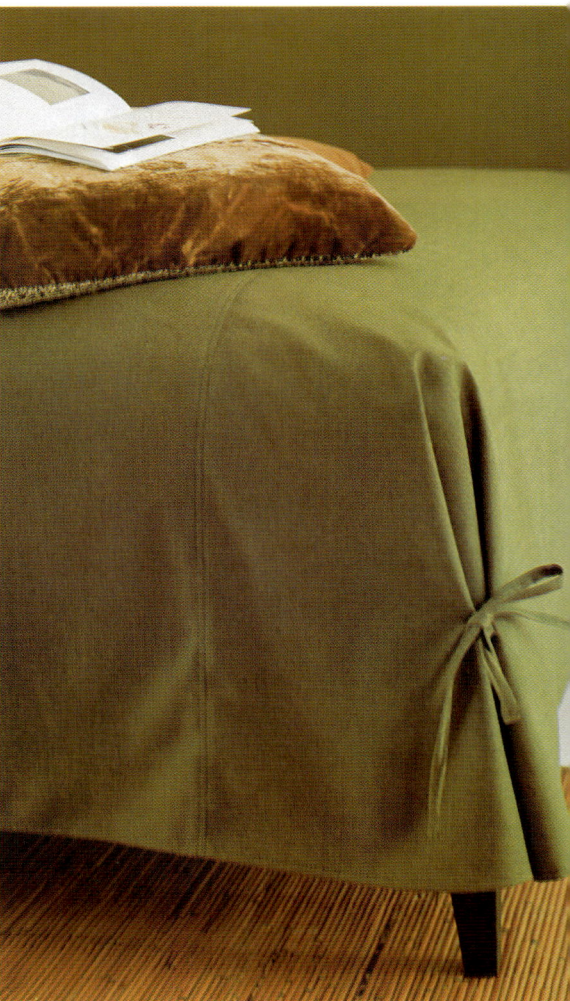

We have referred to two aspects of the decoration process, budget and room dimensions, which though important, are not in the end all that decisive. A large space doesn't have to be filled to the brim at all costs, and the most expensive solution is not necessarily the best.

The combination of wood and raw tones always works. A partition segregates the dressing room. The armchair of Art Déco reminiscences makes a perfect reading spot, and accessories further contribute to the creation of a warm cosy atmosphere. Vases, paintings and an intelligent choice of bedcover and curtain fabrics give any room a personality of its own. Finally, in the case of a large space and limited resources, the loft esthetic comes in handy. Decorative elements here are few but full of character, and the mood is casual.

HEADBOARDS

—The headboard is not necessarily a part of the bed's structure, and it's good to be able to modify it as we please, or change it altogether, without having to deal with the whole bed.

—Light-colored headboards need more care and maintenance than dark-toned ones because constant contact can leave spots and stains.
If one prefers a light color, the headboard should be washable.

a comfortable support

There is nothing like a bad bout of flu to make us stop and consider the importance of the headboard not only as a decorative piece, but also as a functional element. Whatever material it is made of, and whatever its shape, the headboard must meet two basic requirements. First, it must serve as a back that is sturdy and comfortable. Second, it must keep the wall from getting stained. From the most intricate or sophisticated to the simplest of models, perhaps a plain wooden board or two large pillows, headboards play an important role in the bedroom.

After all, they frame both the bed and the things associated with it.

—Headboards that come with the bed's framework have a more categorical, definitive presence and make it unnecessary to rest a separate object against the wall.

—Metallic headboards tend to be purely decorative because they make uncomfortable back supports.
Large pillows that are soft and springy can nevertheless compensate.

—Padded headboards are on the whole the most comfortable. But we must make sure that they are hard enough, as an overly soft support can damage our backs.

HEAD-ON

—The headboard has two purposes: as a support for the body to lean on, and to keep the wall clean.

—A large wooden board placed against the wall can serve as a headboard and embellish one's view of the bed area, concealing the wires of the lamp or the telephone that has been placed on the night table.

—If the board is padded, the upholstery used must have zippers so that it can be easly removed for washing.

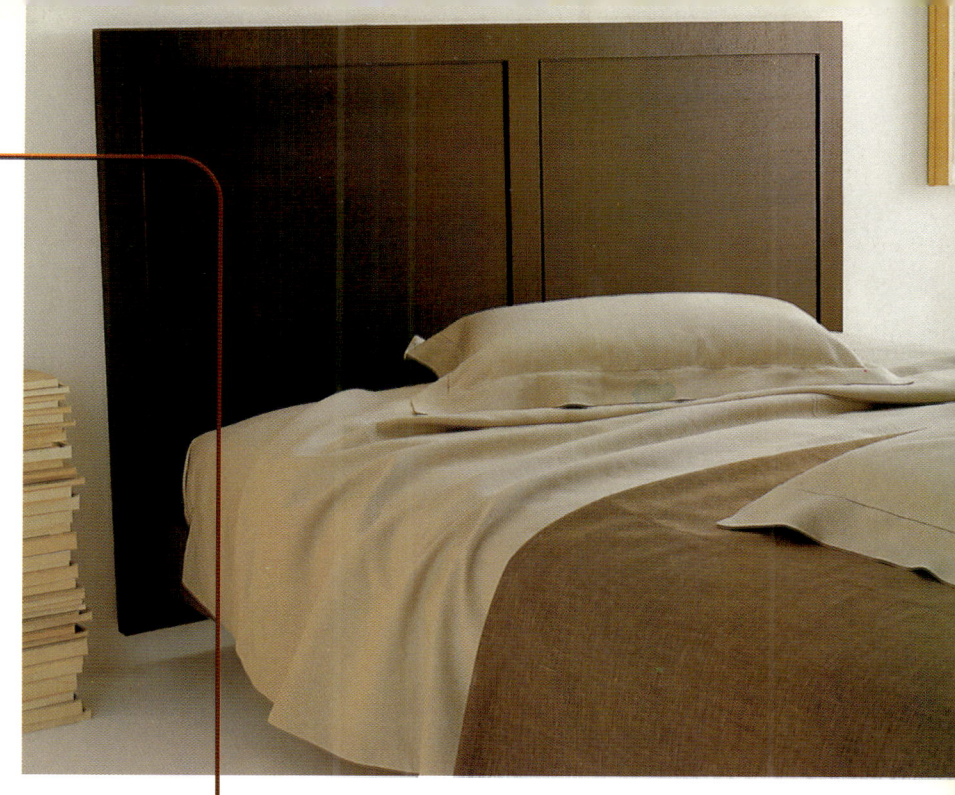

dressing up the bedroom

If the bedroom is in fact an extension of ourselves, we can stretch the idea farther and conclude that just as we dress up ourselves, we must dress up the bedroom. We use the term 'bedclothes' for such things as sheets and pillowcases, so how about the term 'bedroom clothes'? Linguistic reflections aside, it is true that fabrics are as important as the furniture. The bed and the windows are rarely left in the nude. Bedsheets are too intimate to be exposed and the traditional solution is the bed-

cover, which also serves to keep us warm in winter. As for windows, the need for privacy and protection from daylight calls for some kind of screen. When choosing a curtain fabric, one must consider the washing and care it will need, its durability or resistance, and its effectiveness in both hot and cold weather. The latest trends point toward materials that are natural, ecological, soft-toned and richly textured. Whether silk or knitted wool, quality reigns supreme.

in the winter, warm bedroom fabrics will warm up our bodies

Sooner or later summer turns to fall. Temperatures drop, the day shortens. We have to find ways of retaining heat. This does not only mean the comfortable temperature that the heater suddenly permeates our homes with, after months without it. We also need visual and tactile heat if the home is to be a true shelter from the cold, the rain, or simply that frozen air that stings our cheeks. As October approaches, we must get everything ready. The bedroom cannot be exempted from our seasonal preparations. After all, it is a refuge within the larger refuge that the entire home is. Thick bedcovers, heavier drapes, rugs and tapestries that have spent the summer months stored in closets or sent away to the drycleaner's make a reappearance, and the whole bedroom is wrapped up for the winter.

Fabrics are particularly important in rooms that look out to a winter landscape. Sparse and fresh-toned textiles like cotton and linen give way to thicker, warmer ones such as wool and corduroy. Knitted fabrics in particular are an ideal winter material for bedcovers and throw pillows. They are soft, pleasant to the touch, and very, very warm, and they help give the room a relaxed, homey atmosphere. The wide range of textures and patterns possible in knitted fabrics – plain, striped, braids – is something to consider when dressing up a bedroom in neutral tones. If we want color variants, the range becomes infinite. Moreover, knitted fabrics make a good counterpoint when combined with more lavish materials such as velvet or corduroy. Another advantage: they can be washed at home.

Duvets are a wonderful alternative to bedsheets. They vary in thickness, depending on the season. Different colors and patterns allow us to change the look and mood of the bedroom as we please. For those who prefer traditional sheets, the bedcover can suffice to regulate body temperature and give visual variety to the room.

the winter bedroom
tender is the night

When dressing up the bed, one can never go wrong with neutral colors. From whites through creams, grays, ochers and moccas and finally to blacks (too much of which can be rather dramatic), neutral tones are a wonderful option because they are versatile; they even help us to blend in other chromatic options.

Their effect depends on the furniture material. Bright colors and wood have a warming effect on the room, while black has been associated with the high-tech style of the eighties. Associations change, though.

In winter it is safe to go for the bright range of grays and browns, which have the effect of making the room atmosphere warm and cosy, comfortable and inviting.

Mohair, wool and the incredibly soft touch of cashmere in these tones make for calm sweet dreams.

Note the combinations illustrated here: raw colors with metal for an austere design, and black with wood, which is rare but highly evocative.

soft colors, silky fabrics: ready for bed

choosing fabrics

—Priority must go to quality, since a good fabric means greater durability and resistance.

—Bedrooms tend to be designed with winter in mind, but must be cooled down in summer. With two different sets of bedroom clothing we can adapt it to the changes of season.

—Corduroys and wools provide warmth in winter. Since these textiles are very thick, they must be stored away in summer, which is also a good time to have them cleaned.

—When choosing fabrics for the bedroom, it's good to know beforehand what kind of cleaning processes they require. Some textiles need very expensive ones, complicating maintenance altogether.

—Knitted fabrics are wonderful for bedcovers and throw pillows, and give a relaxing, cosy touch to the bedroom. Linen is best in summer because it is light and fresh.

time for bed

—An unattractive bed can be made attractive simply by dressing it up, both in the headboard and along the base, with a textile that goes with the overall decor of the room.

—One solution is the skirt, covering the bed base and underpart. The skirt can be plain or patterned, and of any of a wide range of materials.

—The mattress must have a case and the market offers diverse models: made-to-measure or standard, with zipper or elastics, etc. There are also padded ones that are supposed to stimulate deeper sleep.

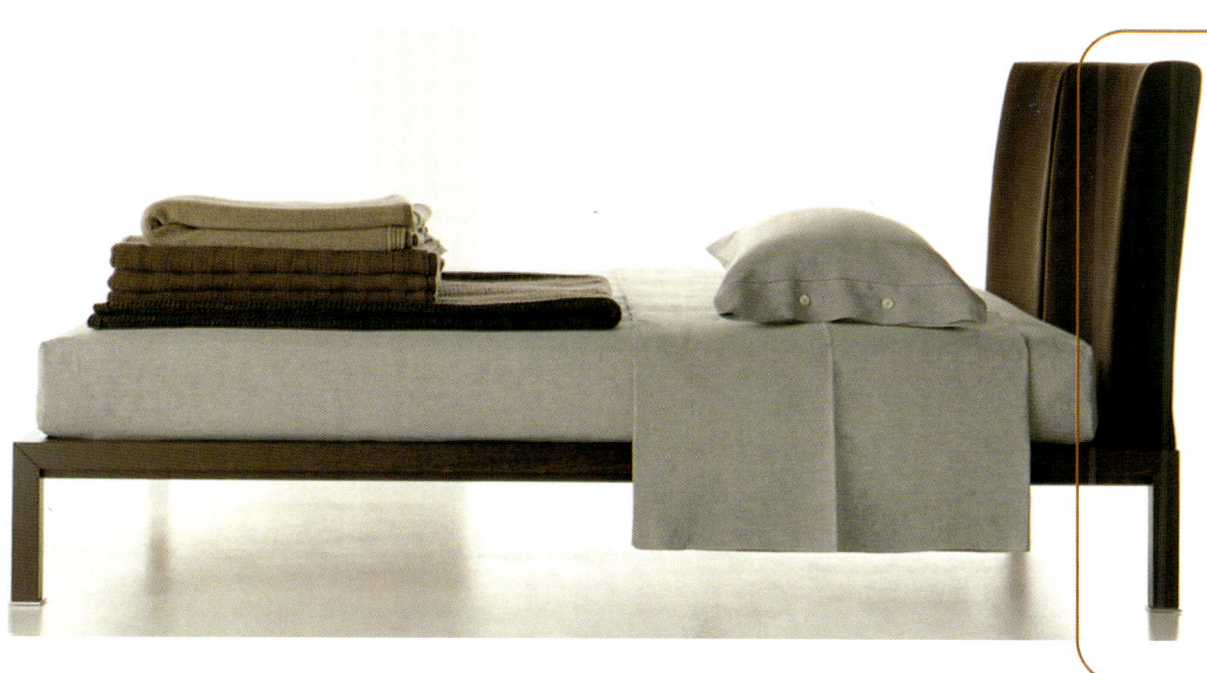

—Quality bedclothing is not a superfluous luxury, but an investment. It has a bearing on the quality of our rest hours, and hence on our overall well-being.

—Warm fabrics are best in winter. Wool and cotton make a good combination.

—If your budget permits, try a bedding set that combines cashmere with silk and ensure yourself a long deep sleep.

—Creams, browns and grays are good colors for winter bedding. They are warmer to the eye and stimulate sleep.

protective mantles
the pleasure of natural fabrics

Beddings are an essential element in the bedroom. Beyond their strictly functional character, tradition attached symbolic value to them. Bedclothing was an important part of a bride's trousseau, its quality and richness testifying to the social status of her family. Nowadays beddings no longer carry such connotations. They are regarded simply by virtue of their usefulness. But this does not mean that quality is no longer taken into account. On the contrary, quality counts more than ever. It was not too long ago that we rediscovered the advantages of natural fabrics, as against the use and abuse of synthetics that the seventies introduced. Time has put things back in place and polyester, fortunately, has given way to cotton and linen. Linen bedsheets were once a privilege to be enjoyed by a few. Thanks to technology, traditional fabrics can be treated in such a way that they turn out more durable and resistant, and no longer have to be ironed. Hence we shouldn't think of quality beddings as an old-fashioned caprice or a legacy of our mothers and grandmothers, but as a long-term investment. High-quality rest means high-quality life.

linen sheets, electric fans, mosquito nets, the color white everywhere...
the summer bedroom and a puff of fresh air

Summer is the time of heat waves, vacations, long afternoons and mosquitoes. Everythings seems to slow down. Our bodies feel heavier, we move more sluggishly, the air feels thick. Of course we are talking about the sticky summers of the south, from Lisbon to Jerusalem. Northern summers in contrast are mild and temperate, as if in compensation for inclement winters. We all know of sleepless summer evenings when the sheets stick to our skins and we long for winter nights under a thick blanket. With the windows closed we are short of air, with the windows open we still feel short of air and the summer street noise keeps us awake.

It is extremely important, therefore, to prepare the bedroom for summer conditions. With a little imagination and especially common sense, we can make it a breathable place. After all, it's our sleep that's at stake.

Air conditioning systems are practical but rather complicated and expensive. An ever-ready alternative is the electric fan, which besides being functional, can be very decorative. Top left, two fifties-style models in pastel colors, small and attractive enough to go on any horizontal surface.

Upholsteries tend to be chosen with winter in mind. When the summer heat comes, we can cover them with fresher textiles like cotton and linen.

The covers can be made-to-measure ones bordered with elastic strips. But we can also simply cut out a piece of cloth the size of the armchair and throw it over, or even tie knots on the sides and back of the couch to hold the fabric in place.

- Cotton is the best fabric with which to dress up the bedroom in summer. It has dethroned linen, an old luxury that nevertheless need not be renounced altogether, being of a quality that is fresh and conducive to rest.

- In the absence of a good air conditioning system, try a fifties-style electric fan, either a ceiling one painted the same color as the walls or a portable one on the chest of drawers or auxiliary table. Besides serving a purpose, a fan can be decorative.

- A gauze mosquito net over the bed keeps out annoying insects when these abound, and gives the room a certain colonial air.

- White is the most refreshing color. Use it for throw pillows and bed clothes, for drapes and upholsteries, and the temperature mellows down, at least visually.

In summer, cotton and linen reign supreme among textiles because they are light and healthy. These fabrics breathe, and allow our bodies to breathe as well. Cotton and linen are therefore the best materials to dress our bedrooms with, and in both color and texture the possibilities are infinite.

A thick, raw, undyed cotton fabric makes a perfect summer bedcover, creating a natural and casual atmosphere. Whether strong or delicate in texture, it is also ideal for throw pillows, drapes, and even armchairs and couches. Then there is canvas, a natural, resistant and very fresh cloth that was ostracized for years but is now once again very popular.

The colonial style is always a reference for hot climates, and an inevitable assocation is the mosquito net. Made of gauze or any other very fine see-through fabric, this element protects us from hungry summer fauna.

AN EFFICIENT AUXILIARY SURFACE

The night table must above all be functional, its type and dimensions depending on how we are to use it.

If we want it as a base for a reading lamp, the sockets shouldn't be too far away from the spot. It is best to keep wires out of sight. If besides a lamp we wish to install an electric alarm clock, a radio or a telephone, pre-planning of outlets becomes even more important.

Another thing to consider is the relation between the table and the lamp. A lamp's arc of light depends on both its base and the surface it stands on. Unless the lamp on it has a particularly tall base, a low table hinders illumination.

An overly high table, on the other hand, makes the reclined person have to sit up when reaching out for something on it. A solution is the night table with two or more horizontal surfaces at different levels.

KLIMT

Antonio Canova

ROY LICHTENSTEIN

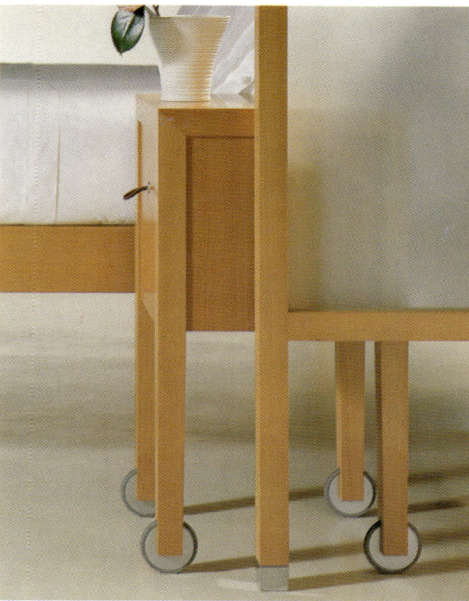
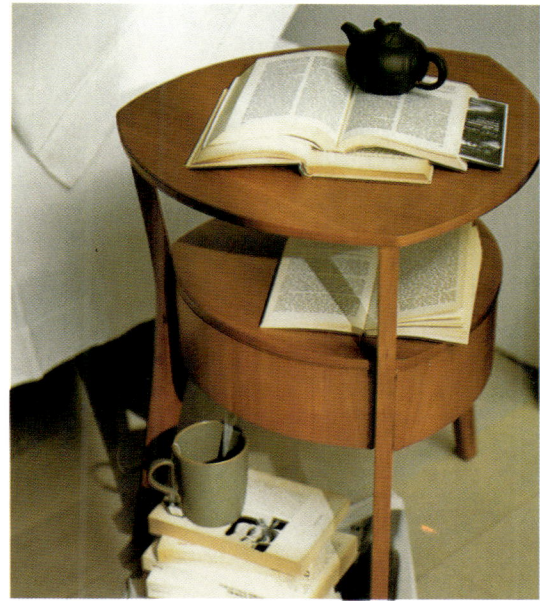

night tables
a good auxiliary surface

The only truly indispensable element in the bedroom is the bed. Nevertheless, the night table plays a very important role. It comes in a wide range of types but its function is always the same: to serve as an auxiliary surface, and often also as a storage surface. Here are six different interpretations of the same concept. Top left, contemporary use of a classical auxiliary table. The top board and the space under it are auxiliary surfaces while the bulk below is a small closet. The legs are tall enough for more objects to be stored in the space underneath.

Top center, a wheeled table that fits perfectly behind the headboard of glass and wood. Top right, table with two horizontal surfaces and a small round closet. Lower left, a wood and metal chest of drawers with wheels for legs serving as a night table. Next to this, a rectangular structure attached to the same wooden board that clads part of the wall. It strikes a contrast with the blue headboard. Finally, a suspended white-lacquered box supports an articulated lamp.

the night table: where we dump everything before surrendering ourselves to the arms of Morpheus

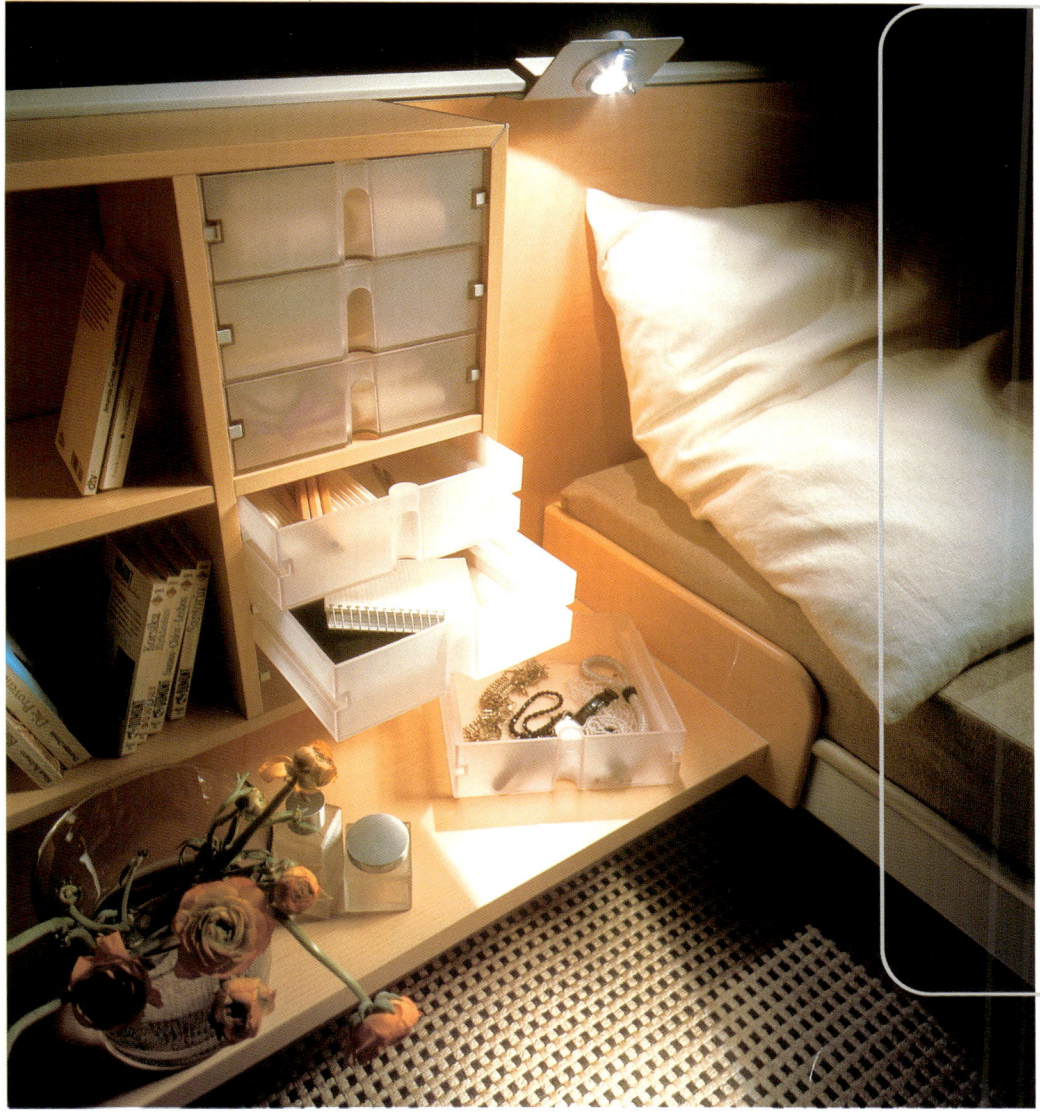

making the most of everything

—When choosing a night table, consider what you will be using it for. To many, a surface on which to place a lamp and a book will suffice.

—Others tend to accumulate a wide assortment of objects beside their beds. In this case go for a table that includes large drawers below.

—In the absence of drawers, the space underneath can be made useful through boxes stacked on the floor.

—The boxes could also go on the table. This is an at once practical and decorative solution.

—Transparent or translucent boxes make their contents easily recognizable, hence contributing to order. Boxes make for original solutions, and visually do not take up space.

The bedroom is a living, organic space and as such is transformable. Our preferences and needs change with time, so that some things go, others are altered, and new ones come into the picture. The night table is no exception. In the course of our lives we accumulate objects almost without realizing it, only to end up not knowing where to keep them. The night table drawer is a domestic container that is particularly likely to get filled with a motley assortment of anarchically accumulated objects. One same drawer eventually juxtaposes invoices, medications, magazines and postcards in a happy but very impractical mess.

The solution is to compartmentalize. In the case of a lone drawer, small boxes can define departments. If the table surface is large enough, a box can actually go on it. This is both practical and decorative.

If there is space in the room for a larger piece of furniture, the night table can be part of a storage module. Here and on the opposite page, the module is an extension of the headboard, and its compartments are translucent. A clock, books, medicines and a personal diary are tidily arranged on the table and hence easy to pick up in the middle of the night when needed.

—The night table can serve as well as a storage piece, especially in a small bedroom. The same space that would be taken up by a board and four legs is used instead for a small chest of drawers.

—Night tables tend to be rather low, making illumination a problem. A good solution is the desk type of lamp with an articulated arm and an adjustable focus.

—Many bed sets come with night tables. When they do not, the secret is to harmonize with the headboard.

—A pull-out tray under the table surface is perfect for breakfast in bed. In the case of smaller budgets, a stool is always a practical temporary solution.

a place for everything: the night table organizes the bed's surroundings

intimate and personal
keys to choosing a night table

As in planning the bedroom as a whole, several factors must be considered when choosing a night table. Individual necessities come first. Whereas one person may need a cabinet in which to store the most varied objects, from letters and mementos to handkerchiefs, medications and sunglasses, another will make do with a board for a lamp and a book. The size and proportions of the bedroom also count. If we have very little space and no large closets, the night table can be a chest of drawers and we can use the drawers for keeping sweaters and underwear. The height of the night table is very important because it has a bearing on the lighting of the bed, as well as on our having or not having to sit up from a lying position when we need to reach out for something. Below, a chest of drawers serving as a night table. The dark tone of the wood contrasts with the whiteness of the bed and gives a certain character to the room. The design is original, with the fronts of the drawers glazed to reveal their contents. The key to achieving a harmonious composition is a fluid dialogue with the headboard, striking either a balance or a contrast.

Upholstered padded headboards are at once esthetic and comfortable as an extra support for our heads and bodies when we slide into bed.

The padding must neither be too hard nor too soft, and the upholstery should be of a fabric that is easy to wash and pleasant, texture-wise, to the touch.

Above, three very comfortable headboards that blend in perfectly with the atmosphere of the bedroom.

Left, a bed whose frame is upholstered with the same fabric that covers the headboard. Cream tones have a warm and clean look that is inducive to rest.

Center, a headboard padded with soft foam and upholstered with white can-vas. Several throw pillows are dressed with the same fabric in other tones.

Right, a bed of light-colored wood and with a marked geometry that joins the headboard to the night table. In this model, two night tables are connected by a shelf behind the headboard, positioned in such a way as to leave space for it. The dark color of the Alcántara fabric that covers both the headboard and the bed itself strikes a contrast with the light tones of the wood. Dark colors are also more resistant to dirt.

Bottom, a view of the previous model showing the whole ensemble. Minimal decor for an austere but warm environment.

the calm silent atmosphere of austere, almost naked bedrooms

#

Color is one of the main tools used by professional decorators when fitting out a space, whether domestic or public. A good chromatic composition can make a difference. Healthwise, we know that color has an enormous bearing on our state of mind and general wellbeing. In so important a place as the bedroom – which must put us in a relaxed and happy attitude, both mentally and physically, so that it is not only merely beautiful but also 'therapeutic' – color becomes essential. To the purest of purists, white is best, permeating the room with silence and serenity. But with sparse furniture and a minimum of ornaments, painting the walls with a soft color combined with whites and beiges for window and door frames can give the room a stronger personality. Light blues, yellows, terracottas and creams induce rest while cheering up the place.

like a garden
colorful flowers

Why not? In snow-white spaces and austere atmospheres, amid pure forms, there is always room for flowers, patterns and pastel colors – in short, for romanticism. We can revive those cosy, slightly naïve rooms we imagine when we read a Jane Austen novel, though contemporary shapes and combinations will give them a fresh dose of style and funcionality.

Pop furniture can be juxtaposed with curtains and discreet textile prints, creating a refreshing mix. Above, a relaxed atmosphere where yellow and lilac blend in with innovative furniture. The bedcover and the wallpaper pattern would have delighted our grandmothers. Left, new version of the canopied bed, with pastel colors dominating.

The latest tendency is to combine the color white and the pure form with patterns and pastel tones

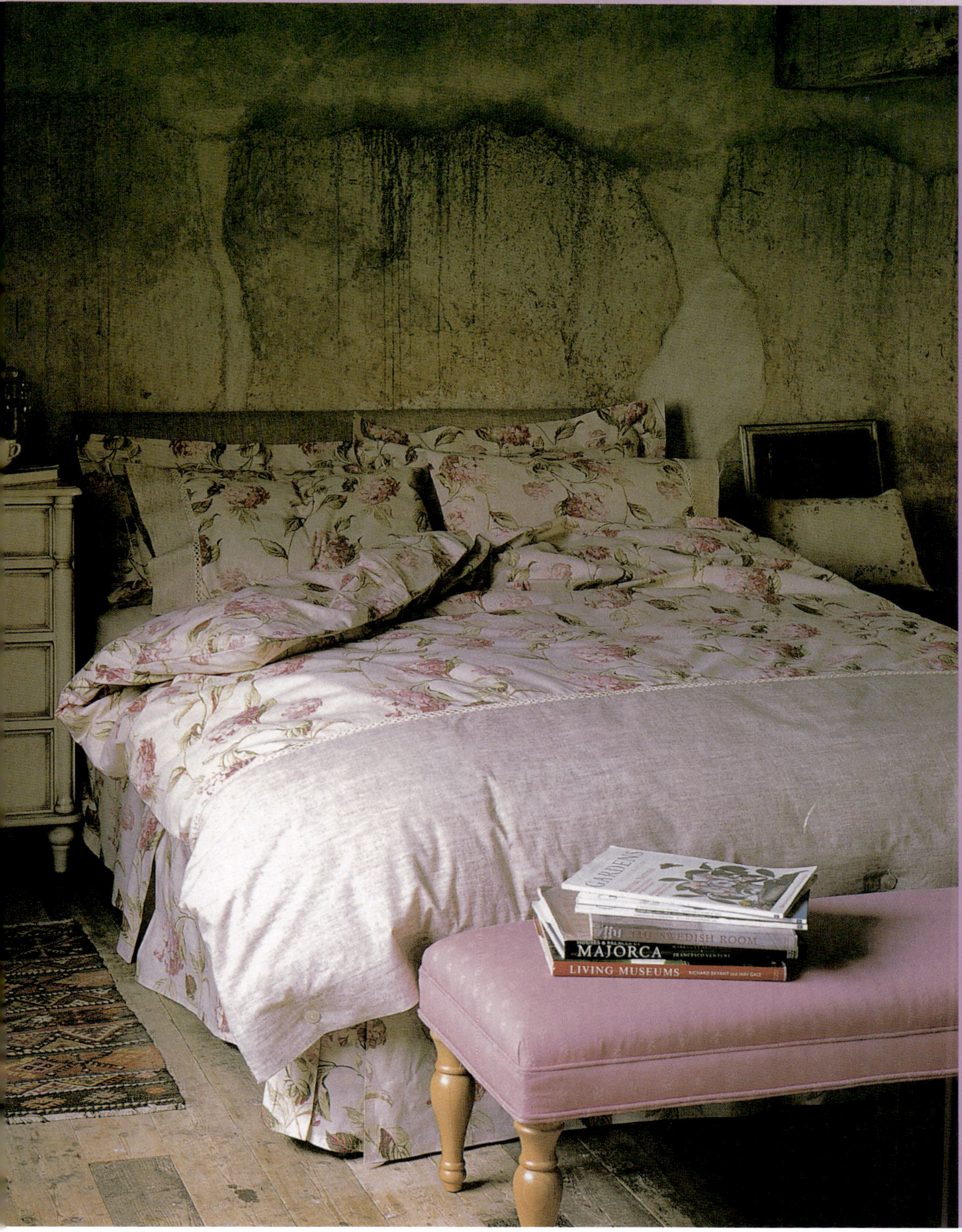

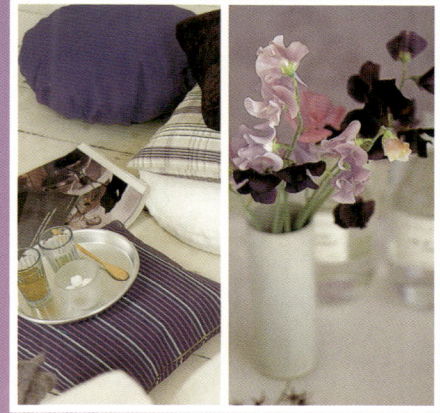

–Painting on wood is an excellent way of giving the room some color and recycling old furniture. To achieve resistant surfaces, the wood must first be sanded. The top coating of paint should have a glossy or a matt finish.

–Washed wood looks perfect in a simple, rustic-style bedroom.

–When choosing fabrics, take into account the colors of the furniture, flooring and walling.

–Fabrics with flower patterns cheer up and brighten up the place. Another way to cheer up a bedroom is by combining different patterns of the same tone (stripes, flowers and checks, for instance). A clashing combination, however, is attractive only at first, if at all. Sooner or later one gets tired of it.

Chromotherapy
special properties of color

Tastes and colors, of course, are a thorny subject, a matter of opinion, and it is not our intention to open up a debate. Nevertheless, a few basic considerations are in order.

Like clothes design, interior decoration is subject to fashions, counterfashions, trends and infinite variants. The sixties, for example, saw the pop and hippy styles flourishing side by side in a mix of the rustic, the eastern and the bazaar. Not all was Warhol, neither was everything Madrás, but both strongly influenced the mood of those years. Returning to the matter of color, undoubtedly the nineties have been witness to a heyday of natural and neutral tones, a boom of minimalist decor marked by the absence of chromatic dispays. But it is also evident that the color fever has reared its head anew, through prominent activists like Tricia Guild. In other words the options are infinite, the sky's the limit.

Still, some age-old common sense maxims will always hold: dark colors shrink spaces whereas light colors create breadth. As for patterns, the larger they are, the more they reduce space. Cold colors are aseptic while warm ones create a sensation of life and energy. One final recommendation: the ultimate choice is the consumer's.

—Colors can be classified into two broad groups: warm and cold. The warm colors are red, orange, yellow and their corresponding nuances and tones. Included here are browns, earth tones, ochers and their own respective nuances. Warm colors are said to produce, precisely, a feeling of warmth and closeness. The cold colors include greens, blues and purples.

—A final note: light colors are more easily soiled. When choosing fabrics, one must be sure about washing instructions.

—Warm colors make spaces seem smaller, cosier and more cluttered, as against cold colors which have the effect of enlarging and unburdening them. When deciding on a range of colors to decorate the bedroom with, it is important to consider its optical effect.

—Black and white must be considered separately. Their effect on the eye must also be taken into account when combining them. White enlarges space whereas black does the opposite.

black & *white*

Black and white together make the the most classical of color combinations. They are diametrically opposed, of radically different natures. White reflects all the light it receives, whereas black absorbs it completely. Hence they were always meant for each other.

The traditional marriage of black and white was neither casual nor innocent. Currents like Op Art long exploited the optical effects produced by the mix of the two colors. The common chessboard floor is a good example of how these effects were used in the field of interior decoration. The combination of black and white confers elegance and a strong personality on any kind of space.

The question is how to combine them. One must guard against bringing in too many other colors. An unwritten rule has black and white necessarily excluding the presence or proximity of other colors, which otherwise destroy the perfect contrast between them. An exception here is gray, which comes from mixing the two. Gray serves to soften the contrast between black and white, resulting in greater harmony and balance. The combination of black and white had its heyday in the eighties, a decade we associate with a cold technological style. The association still holds today, as we can see on this page, but it is now also good to bring in wood, which helps create a warmer, friendlier atmopshere.

—The combination of black and white is the most classical of chromatic tandems. Its elegance, its simplicity and the infinite possibilities it offers have made it the queen of color alliances.

—An important aspect of this combination is its optical effect. This was one of the pillars of Op Art, an artistic current born halfway through the century which sought to explore and exploit the optical and visual effects of color combinations. We can apply such effects when decorating the bedroom.

— Chromatic variety in a room enhances shapes and textures. The geometries and contours of individual elements are more clearly defined and volumes stand out in all their splendor.

white reflects light, black absorbs it
and together they trigger a vibrant spatial play

white on white
a bedroom bathed in light

White is the complete color – or the anticolor, as we please, symbolizing that which is pure, hygienic, immaculate. It is the color that best reflects light and most produces a sense of breadth. For these very reasons, some people avoid it when decorating a room. It may be clean, they say, but also cold.

Here we wish to promote complete white as the ideal chromatic choice, to strip it of its alleged frozenness or clinical asepsis and give it the place it deserves in the field of decoration.

Light is a factor to take into account when using the color white, for nothing injects life to an immaculate space as a good inflow of daylight does.

The absence of color in a room has the effect of enhancing the exterior, with windows acting as frames through which the landscape enters and enriches the interior.

Finally, the predominance of white in furniture and fabrics makes other elements of the bedroom stand out. Decorative pieces like a painting, a tapestry or even a vase take on a special meaning, one that a greater presence of color around would most likely deprive them of.

Below, a bedroom rendered in white. A large headboard lords it over and gives the room a strong personality. The space is totally stripped of decor and hence functions as a true temple of repose, a void that induces relaxation and the abandonment of everyday problems, a bubble of peace and quiet.

the peaceful house

–White is a color with therapeutic powers. Its neutrality and capacity to absorb light makes it a powerful device with which to create peaceful and relaxing, bright and fresh atmospheres.

–The wood of the bedframe and night tables is enhanced against the predominant snow-white of the walls and beddings. The colors of the few objects there are around become more vibrant and beautiful.

red, yellow, blue... colors can radically change one's perception of space

CAPITALIZING ON COLOR

—The most insipid space can undergo a radical transformation through an intelligent combination of colors on the walls, floors and frames.

—Light colors magnify a space, dark ones shrink it. Vivid colors give life and movement to a room, whereas duller colors induce peace and calm.

—There are no set rules to follow when combining colors. We must not adhere to preconceived ideas, nor be afraid to experiment, but give free rein to our creativity and come up with our own living space.

—The primary colors — red, blue and yellow — transform spaces by injecting them with movement, vivacity and energy. These are vibrant colors with strong personalities.

—There is nothing like red to cheer up a bedroom. A touch of it here and there suffices to transform the entire character of the room.

—Blue has relaxation-inducing properties, and like yellow, it helps illuminate the room.

sweet flavors
soft colors for fresh atmospheres

Music tames beasts, pastel colors appease the spirit. We all know of the relaxation-inducing, soothing, pacifying properties of these tones. Pastels are not colors but tones one gets when a color is diluted in white. We come up with harmonious, refreshing compositions like sky blue, light green, soft yellow or pink when we put bright blues, greens, yellows and reds through a filter of white.

Pastel colors had their heyday in the fifities. In the wake of the Second World War, the United States indulged in the American dream. Modernity, comfort, technological advance and economic prosperity made Americans look to the future with optimism. And pastel colors were the backdrop of this happy decade.

The photographs on this page show how soft colors can create a fresh airy atmosphere. Above: sash windows brightening up an entire room, Scandinavian airs for a bedroom dominated by the color blue, duvet with a cover checked in several tones of blue, armchair upholstered in white cotton, and the simplest of night tables. Right, a composition whose freshness comes from the combination of light tones. A chest at the foot of the bed provides a touch of the old days.

natural light
the fifth element

Natural light is not something that is always at our disposal, but there are mechanisms by which to make the most of it when on hand. It is important to know what direction the rooms of the house face and what time each one is blessed by the sun. Geography also has a bearing on the amount and intensity of daylight received. It's one thing to live north, another to live south. Northerners must make the most of any daylight received, whereas southerners also have to protect themselves from it. Right, a practically toplit attic bedroom. A curtain hanging from a bar set two-thirds up the window serves to filter the incoming light. Below right, two large wooden-framed windows deprived of curtains so as to let daylight shine in profusely. Bare windows take on the role of paintings, framing the landscape so that it becomes part of the room's decoration, so that the exterior enters the interior.

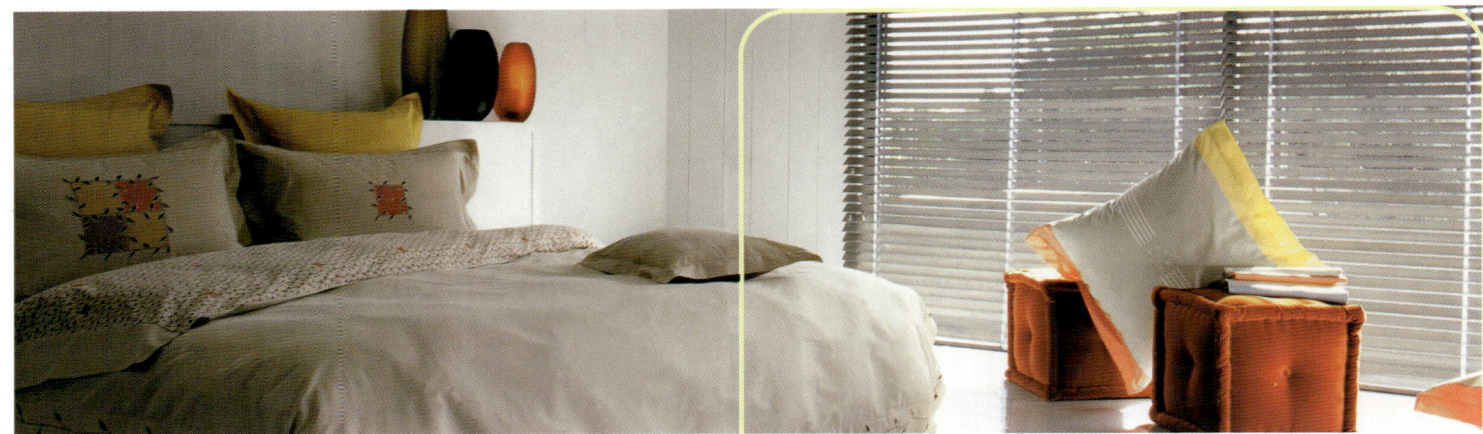

HOW TO CHOOSE:

—When deciding on curtains or blinds, first consider the kind of lighting you want for the room. If the idea is to maximize the inflow of daylight, go for net or lace curtains, roller blinds or Venetian blinds. If you need a dimmer atmosphere, thick drapes are the solution.

—The double curtain is a practical option that gives us both privacy and a feeling of closedness. A thin net or lace curtain lets light in, while a heavier, more opaque one keeps both light and noise out when desired.
Once your choice is made, proceed to plan how to install it. There is a whole range of systems available, but the most common are guides and bars, which in themselves can be decorative.

There is no better way to make a room a peaceful, warm and luminous space than by making light predominate it, bathing each and every corner and changing as the day goes by. But we also need a minimum of privacy and closedness. Net or lace curtains help produce the right interaction between exterior and interior, between the busy world of the street and our own private world. They let sunlight filter in but protect us at the same time. They are fresh, weightless, and easy to combine with other elements of the bedroom. Once we have brought light into the room, we must enhance it. Cream colors are both luminous and warm, besides giving a sense of breadth.

The pictures here show a bedroom with an original night table whose sides, having pockets, perform the function of drawers.

The room is stripped of all superfluous details, so that each and every element that there is becomes important. There is a notable mix of styles in the furnishing, with a modern bed of light-colored wood blending in with a dressing table and two antique closets of dark wood. The lace curtains hang from a simple bar of painted iron.

soft light, fresh air, comfortable pillows and a cup of tea on the night table

a cosy
atmosphere

It doesn't take much to create a cosy, safe-feeling, intimate and relaxed atmosphere – a place, in sum, where one feels at home. Here are four examples. The preceding page shows a composition in white, off-white and black, with the bed and the night tables engaged in a play of opposites. The bed is white, the tables black. The play is repeated here and there, with a particularly strong chromatic contrast between the night tables and the radiantly white lamps on them. There are never any clashes, however, because the pureness of the lines, in fact the overall harmonious geometry of the room, has a soothing effect.

Above, two seemingly disparate proposals which actually come from one same design concept: a clean space stripped of all superfluous elements and rendered in relaxing, neutral colors.

Right, a bedroom which has made natural light its main ally, and the optimization of space its decorative virtue and objective.

In the quest for comfort and a cosy atmosphere in the bedroom, try going back in time and resorting to classical furniture, fine wood and colonial style.

Classical is not to be equated with cluttered, nor with massive, much less with solemn. Colonial style, in turn, refers to an esthetic that arose from the combination of styles prevailing in European metropoli from the mid-19th century on, with the decorative and constructive elements characteristic of its colonies.

Opposite page, a classical bedroom with colonial influences. The bed is of fine wood and simple sinuous shapes. A chest at the foot of the bed transports us to another era and unknown places. To the left on this page, a bed with a canopy and mosquito netting. Next in clockwise direction, a classical bedroom livened up with a profusion of flowers. Beside this, a serene composition in which wood reigns supreme. To its left, ethnic influences in a brightly colored kilim that provides a counterpoint to the bare essentiality of the rest of the furnishing. Right, African airs for a very bright bedroom.

In an attic, make low furniture occupy the low areas and leave the higher spaces free. Exposed beams create a cosy and original atmosphere, especially when left in their natural color. Badly lit attics must be given light colors, which also have the effect of magnifying the space, as in the picture to the right.

How nice life would be if we were completely free to choose the space we are to inhabit, with no restrictions whatsoever! Unfortunately, reality mostly has us having to make do with what there is, not only in terms of dimensions but also in terms of layout.

We owe it to ourselves to at least try to make the most of what the circumstances of our lives offer. Calm is of the essence. For any seemingly impossible situation, there is a clever remedy. Above, an attic turned into a cosy, comfortable bedroom. An intelligent combination of colors is the key to a miracle: yellow-painted walls make the room nice and bright, and red gives it life and energy. The bed features wrought iron at its best. With the help of its white color, it exudes a sense of lightness and luminosity. Left, attic with exposed wooden beams. These have been left in their natural color so as to highlight the whiteness of the surroundings and hence both enhance and enlarge the space.

—Corners tend to go to waste, but can be extremely useful extra spaces.

—To capitalize on such seemingly useless areas, try furniture like a corner module or right-angles shelves.

—Mirrors magnify a small space visually and multiply the light in it. They can serve as closet doors or coat an entire wall.

—When a room is long and narrow, varying the floor level helps to break the feeling of infinity and make the room more kinetic in different directions. A platform near the window, by creating two areas in one, can have the effect of widening the room.

difficult spaces

What can we do with a long narrow room so that it doesn't look like a corridor? Shorten and widen the space. How? Through a visual effect. It's amazing how easily we are deceived by the eye. A white square will look larger to us than a black square of the same dimensions, and this is nothing compared to other tricks of the eye.

Here are some for the long narrow bedroom. The short far-end walls can be painted darker than the long side ones, or perhaps lined with bookcases, closets or any other elements that eat up space. We could also terrace the space, as in the bedroom shown on the right. The floor is raised near the window, resulting in a more dynamic room while creating a little sitting or reading area.

Above, a problem of dimensions tackled without recourse to the well-tried white solution. Here red and black give the room a dynamic, vibrant quality, with the absence of superfluous decor making possible the optimization of space.

Another widely used trick in the case of limited space is the mirror. Mirrors multiply light, enlarge space, and come in handy when we dress ourselves up.

Mirrors come in many shapes: flat, beveled, round, as closet doors. Our choice will be what best combines with the rest of the room.

Below this caption: to maximize the visual effect of the mirror, it covers the entire front of a wall-to-wall closet. Besides being an architectural device that enlarges a room's sense of breadth, the mirror is a good thing to have when we dress up in the bedroom or go about our ablutions in the bathroom.

The main compensation for limited space is imagination. With a bit of inventiveness and organization, there is almost always some solution. It's important to consider all alternatives, no matter how adventurous some may seem.

Doors can be real headaches in small rooms. If they open inward, they take up precious space.

In this case, why not change the system altogether? Sliding doors are a good solution. Shown here is a bedroom in which wood is the dominant material. The walls are lined with light-colored timber, giving the room a sense of warmth and uniformity. Being of the same material, the sliding door merges with the wall when closed.

On the floor
futons and low beds

We have previously mentioned the growing eastern influences in the way we decorate our interiors. If there is a country that is a constant reference in the language of interior design, it is Japan.

The Zen esthetic sums up the tendencies of this turn-of-millennium, namely simplicity, austerity, minimalism, harmony and contact with nature, tendencies which are fast gaining ground.

So the Orient has conquered even our bedrooms, with the futon at the forefront. The futon is a mattress quilted with cotton, alone or mixed with latex or coconut fiber (all natural materials). It is one of the best things to sleep on. The traditional thing is to spread it out on a tatami, which is a low platform made of a mat material. In the morning it is rolled up and kept aside. In Western environments the futon tends to be laid on a different kind of support, any of many possibilities, and stays there more permanently. The futon goes with austere atmospheres, in rooms stripped of superfluous decor, often where the dominant material is wood, the warmth of which makes up for the bareness.

The advantages of the futon are not merely esthetic. The materials it is made of are totally ecological, as well as healthy for the back. It must be aired and sunned with frequency.

Right, a very cosy bedroom with exposed wooden beams and much of the floor covered with blocks of tatami. The futon is spread on one of them, beneath a small, cube-shaped skylight.

—The futon is totally natural and ecological. Being a thin mattress, it is very healthy for the spinal column.

—Being made of natural materials, the futon needs to breathe. It must be taken outdoors frequently enough for sunning and airing. In this way the fibers are oxygenated and the materials obtain their original freshness and thickness.

—A wooden board will do in the absence of a tatami, though the futon could actually also go on the frame of a regular bed, as if it were a regular mattress. See to it, however, that the base of the bed is neither of slats nor of springs, but a simple wooden board. Otherwise the futon will get deformed.

—Don't make mistakes here. A futon is not a regular mattress. It must be spread on a tatami, or at least a hard continuous flat surface. Otherwise its advantages go to waste.

tidy rooms
tricks to keep the bedroom neat

To keep everything tidy and in place, it helps to consider in advance what assortment of belongings will be coming into the house, and then where we wish to put each one. Pre-planning is essential if we wish to avoid unpleasant surprises later.

On this page, the closets are camouflaged to one side of the bed, merging with the walls through color and the absence of door knobs or handles. The shelf above the closets breaks the vertical rhythm of their doors. Beyond the foot of the bed, under the white window 'counter', a collection of wicker baskets helps to keep the place uncluttered while exuding a touch of warmth.

A PLACE FOR EVERYTHING

—Dressing rooms give a lot of leeway. Storage can be concentrated in them so that the main space of the bedroom is exclusively for rest and relaxation.

—Let's not disdain solutions like chests of drawers, closets and shoeracks. Boxes of cardboard, wood or wicker can stand in for drawers, and in the absence of closets, try those structures that shops use to display clothes on. The problem here is dust. Cleaning becomes fundamental when the wardrobe is exposed.

—To make the bedroom look and feel larger, the dressing room can be delimited by a simple glazed screen. Besides looking good, this would let light into all corners.

—Without a shoerack, shelves in any corner will do.

—The wardrobe -clothes, shoes and accessories- takes up a considerable amount of space. In the absence of a separate dressing room, it must go into the actual bedroom, and this requires thought and imagination. The idea is to make the most of what there is.

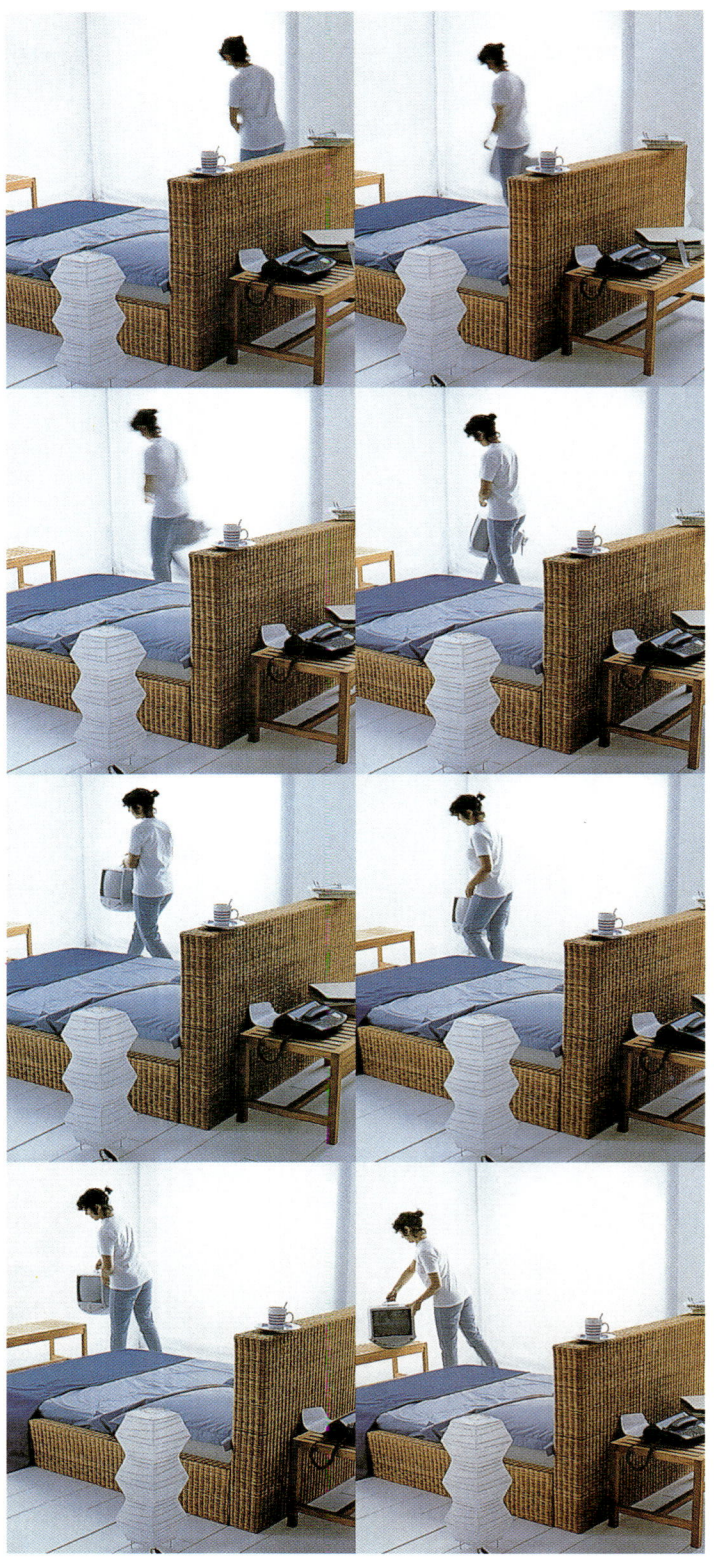

Order: systematic arrangement or placing of things, in such a way that each takes up the space it is assigned to. Theoretically a simple matter of system and organization, but easier said than done. Practice proves it difficult to have each object always where it should be. It's like putting the feats of Hercules on the level of a child's game. There is a cyclical evolution from order to disorder (and often too from disorder to outright chaos) and back again. Remember a forgotten time in the past, in our childhood, when the nursery was a logical display of toys that would eventually degenerate into a happy mess. How long does it take the bedroom to drop from near-perfection to anarchy? For some, a matter of months. For others, a couple of days. We have discussed closets, but there is more to order than hanging clothes and keeping pairs of shoes together. The bedroom is a living space where things are constantly happening, where objects are continuously being moved and left around temporarily – on the couch, on the chest of drawers, in the drawer of the night table. It is very important to give each thing a definitive place of its own within the room, which then takes on the nature of a logical, orderly whole.

In the homes of inveterate readers, even the bedroom ends up getting invaded by books. Shelves like the ones shown on this page can help to keep the room uncluttered. The wall that separates the bedroom from the next room serves as a bookcase and a headboard. Two niches at the bottom of the bookcase, flanking the bed, stand in as night tables. The module also provides for the clamping of two reading lamps. The lowest shelf features photographs, giving a personal, more intimate note to the room.

This is indeed a most practical solution. We rarely use the wall surface over our bed, and yet with a bit of imagination it gives so much scope for action. The dominantly neutral colors here further contribute to the creation of a large-looking, uncluttered space.

One last note: people who are allergic to dust and mites must not accumulate too many books in their bedrooms.

first aid
auxiliary furniture in the bedroom

All too often when we arrive home and 'unload', everything gets thrown on the bed – clothes, bags, briefcases, books. Its large horizontal surface invites this. Yet there is a whole range of auxiliary furniture we can use for the purpose. The ultimate idea is to make things easier, as well as more esthetic. Left, a simple table of pure geometries which can serve as a desk. A uniquely placed drawer gives it character and provides a place with which to keep papers and desk objects out of sight. Above, a wooden table with a metal frame and a drawer. Situated at the foot of the bed, it's a perfect spot for a small television set, a flower vase, or anything on hand that we don't yet know where to put... Next page, a wooden chest of drawers with a simple emphatic geometry. Finally, two alternatives to the classical valet: for a large room, a comfortable armchair; for a small one, a wooden bar along the wall. The latter takes up no space and yet several pieces of clothing can neatly hang from it.

Auxiliary furniture elements are by nature versatile. In the bedroom they serve different purposes, according to the needs of each moment. Hence a stool can suddenly become a night table, or a makeshift shelf for books we don't know where to put, a pedestal for a vase full of flowers, or simply a thing to temporarily throw clothes on.

Hence an auxiliary table is a good thing to have in the bedroom, not so much as a decorative element but as a multipurpose item we should make the most of. Functionality aside, however, the auxiliary table must be at least esthetically related to the rest of the bedroom furnishing. Contrasts of style always prove interesting, as well as mixes of old and new. An antique wooden chest can be the perfect counterpoint to a functional bare space.

Shown here is an upholstered bench that can be placed at the foot of the bed to serve as a seat or as a surface to temporarily pile clothes on.

a rocking chair, a divan and a side table can do much to make the bedroom
a more lived-in place during the day

One disadvantage of city life is lack of space, with all the problems this brings. A few fortunate ones have a blank check in the form of surplus square meters, but most people are forced to stop and think how to fit a whole wardrobe and other belongings in a bedroom and not impinge on the sense of peace that is necessary in a space of this kind. The built-in closet is the king of camouflage. If its exterior is merged with the walls of the room, no one need imagine what is hidden behind. For an even greater sense of bareness, breadth or spatiousness, try mirrors, which also enhance lighting and engage us in optical games. This spread shows a large bedroom in which these mirror effects have been obtained. The main decorative elements are the actual volumes and colors.

A huge headboard is perforated on the side to form a little niche for books. Its yellow color – of the same tone as the bed's simple frame – contrasts with the white and blue of the bedcover. Standing out in the nakedness of the room is a chair of leather and curved metal tubes, Mies van der Rohe's Brno model.

the bedroom
of the littlest ones

Children have the same needs as adults: comfort, warmth, privacy and order. But they have additional requirements having to do with such things as safety, and must be provided with storage space for toys and games. Extra imagination is in order. We shall try to address these needs here, so that the bedroom of the resident princes and princesses is as practical, safe and cheerful as possible.

Colors play a key role in the children's bedroom. There is a tendency to graduate intensities according to the age of a child. Newborn babies are given soft, gentle pastel tones, and a few years later their rooms are repainted in happy and fun bright colors. It is important to stimulate the imagination of children, and bright colors have a bearing on how they look at the larger world beyond. Order is also important. A child accumulates toys, which have to be kept somewhere. Baskets and boxes are ever-ready allies for this purpose.

Another thing to remember when planning a child's bedroom is that children grow. What is perfect for a one-year-old will no longer be so in two years' time. It is important to look ahead if the room is to be easily adjustable to the changing needs of the child.

Then there is the safety factor to keep in mind when we choose shapes and materials. Avoid sharp edges, hard surfaces and any other potentially dangerous elements.

small **scale**

—Children are small. This may sound obvious, but must not be taken for granted. Absolutely everything in the child's bedroom, from furniture to structural elements, must be adapted to his or her height.

—Two-year-olds can begin to sleep on standard beds, but other furniture must continue to be at the scale of the child. Tables, chairs and even closet doorknobs must be such that the children can move about with a certain independence and feel they are able to do things on their own.

—If the bed has a metal structure, see to it that all the edges are blunted.

—In the case of a tight budget, the best solution for the early years is a crib which, through changing accessories, adapts to the growth of the child.

Left, child's bedroom with soft color tones. The light blue paint of the wooden furniture brightens up the place, which receives sunshine through a large window. The room is airy and relaxing, with a wooden floor that has a warm, cosy effect. As a chromatic counterpoint, an armchair upholstered with a fabric of red and blue checks redefines the scale of the bedroom, adapting it to the world of children.

In the picture to the right, color is the protagonist. Amongst the toys in a basket at the corner is an extra blanket that the child can pull out on especially cold nights. To guard against colds it must be of a smooth but warm fabric.

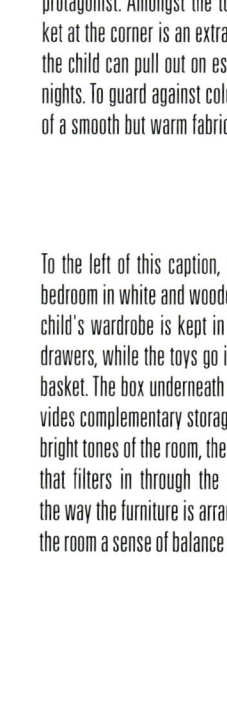
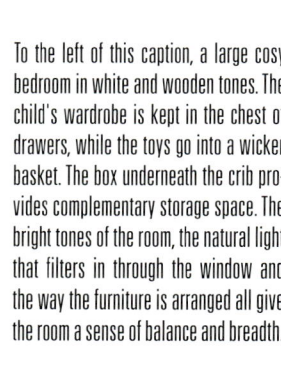

To the left of this caption, a large cosy bedroom in white and wooden tones. The child's wardrobe is kept in the chest of drawers, while the toys go into a wicker basket. The box underneath the crib provides complementary storage space. The bright tones of the room, the natural light that filters in through the window and the way the furniture is arranged all give the room a sense of balance and breadth.

Opposite page, a house where spatial continuity applies as well to the child's bedroom. The built-in closet with pastel green doors creates a special space for the bed, enhancing privacy. A rug delimits and frames the room, besides helping to keep it warm.
The rug also makes a perfect play area.

Left, smooth fabrics cheerfully checkered in red and white, a very youthful pattern that gives life to the bedroom. When planning the child's bedroom, remember that a mere change of bed cover or duvet can change the look of the room entirely, besides adapting it to changing weather conditions and the child's own ever-changing needs.

With an intelligent combination of colors, the most anodyne room can become a happy and cosy place. Contrasts make for vividness, whereas light pastel tones create a more tranquil atmosphere. Red, white and blue is a combination that always works. Besides being esthetic, this mix of colors stimulates children's chromatic percetion.

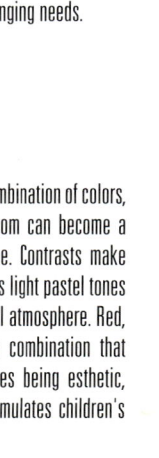

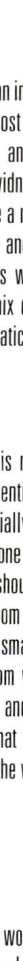

Color is not limited to fabrics. We can color entire rooms as we please, and especially the children's. Whatever color one chooses for the walls, however, it should not be too dark. Otherwise the room loses out on luminosity and looks smaller than it is. Left, a simple bedroom with wooden furniture, yellow walls, and a red niche for books and toys that breaks the chromatic continuity of the walls.

Right, wood combined with cheerfully patterned fabrics. The motif is repeated throughout the room: on the bed, in the curtains, even on the wall. This is an attic, so the aim in planning the room was to optimize space and provide good lighting. Both objectives have been attained through the arrangement of furniture and the choice of colors.

a multi-purpose couch

When coordinating the elements of a bedroom, proceed in such a way that a future change in any one of them will not invalidate the rest. The more independent each element, the more flexible it is. This is particularly important in the case of a child's bedroom; children change fast, and with them their rooms.

We have already seen how a room is transformed with a mere change of fabrics. A weightier issue is furniture. With a bit of imagination, everything is recyclable and recoverable. Children grow, but each spurt upward need not mean a drastic bedroom overhaul. We could at each phase keep part of the furniture as it is, and perhaps adapt it to the child's age.

Shown here is a splendid example of how the couch is adaptable to changing circumstances. It comes in handy when a baby has to be put to sleep or when it's time for a diaper change, or even as something for us to lounge in while the toddler plays. Later on it can take on the functions of a full-fledged sofa-bed, for occasional guests or simply as a thing to relax on.

in order

The littlest members of the household live in a compact, concentrated world. Their bedroom is their world, a small world where everything fits: clothes, toys, school books, their most prized possessions - whether a stone or a piece of string. With such an accumulation of objects, the pressing problem is where to keep it all?

The first thing is not to panic: with a bit of patience and ingenuity, there is a solution for everything. The next is to separate clothes from toys. Clothes go into a closet or a chest of drawers. The more organized the wardrobe, the better, because the child can then acquire the habits of a tidy person, and locate each article more easily as he grows up. Toys are best stored in chests or boxes of any of a wide range of materials. Children must learn to keep their toys early on, so that they don't get used to living in a mess.

Shown here are some examples of the fight against disorder. Hooks on the wall come in handy for the clothes one needs after a bath. Shelves double as shoe storage, and when the child is a bit older they can be used for books or toys. Any kind of box is good for toys. Plastic ones are practical (light, washable, and often dismountable), but also decorative.

So that they don't take up too much space, we can keep boxes out of the way, at the foot of the bed or under the stairs.

the
guest room

Not all homes have a spare room meant exclusively for people who sleep over. More often than not, guests are accommodated in the studio, in one of the children's bedrooms, even in the living room, on the couch. But if there is enough space for an extra room, a guestroom always comes in handy. Knowing there is one, friends will visit more frequently. This room must have some storage space besides a large enough bed, and if possible, also a sitting area and work surface, even if only a simple chair and table.

Since it is not meant for any specific person, the guestroom does not get the same treatment as the rest of the house. But this does not mean that it should be a de-personalized space.

—Ideally it should have a bed, a table, a chair or armchair, and two light fixtures - one general, the other for reading. Think of the guest's comfort.

—If the house is small and the room is assigned other uses, an obvious solution is the sofa-bed. The market offers nice models, that are excellent in both their functions, and with simple opening and closing mechanisms.

—Another option for limited spaces is the futon. It doesn't take up space when rolled up, and when spread on the floor at night it makes a very comfortable bed.

—The guestroom need not be large. Good planning can help keep dimensions and budgets in check.

Index

Acknowledgements

MANUFACTURERS & DESIGNERS

B&B Italia Spa (22060 Novedrate (Co) Italia. Tel. 39-031-795 111. Fax 39-031-791 592. E-mail: beb@bebitalia.it); **Biggie Best** (109 South Liberty Lane, Bristol. Tel. 44-117-9872722. Fax 44-171-9872744); **Cassina Spa** (Via Busnelli, 1. 20036 Meda (Milano) Italia. Tel. 39-0362-3721. Fax 39-0362-34 1510. www.cassina.it); **Christophe Pillet** (81, rue Saint Maur. 75011 Paris, France. Tel. 33-01-48067831. Fax 33-01-48067832); **Culti Agrati SRL** (20030 Seveso, Milano, Italia. Tel. 39-0362-55 19 85. Fax 39-0362-55 14 20); **David Fusseneger textil GesmbH** (A-6850 Dornbirn, Austria. Tel. 43-55 72-228 28. Fax. 43-5572-248 02); **De Tongue** (06560 Valbonne. Tel. 33-4-93958000. Fax 33-4-93654043); **Disform** (Balmes, 71. 08440 Cardedeu (Barcelona) España. Tel. 34-93-846 24 37. Fax 34-93-871 17 67); **Do+Ce** (Avenida Dr. Waksman, 33-39. 46006 Valencia, España. Tel. 34-96-374 26 94. Fax. 34-96-374 07 48); **Descamps España** (www.descamps.com. 08140-Caldes de Montbui, Barcelona, España. Tel. 34-93-862 6622. Fax. 34-93-862 65 15); **Designers Guild** (Head office: 3 Olaf Street, London W11 4BE, England. Tel. 44-171-243 73 00. Fax 44-171-243 73 20); **Donaldson** (NSW 2010 Sydney, Australia. Tel. 9383/9388. Fax 9383/9354); **Elitis** (2bis rue Jean Rodier. 31400 Toulouse. Tel. 33-61 802020. Fax 33-61 809900); **É de Padova** (20121 Milano, Italia, Tel. 39-02-76 00 84 13. Fax 39-02 783 201); **Habitat** (1, Place Royale, 78230 Le Pecq, France); **Ikea España** (28023 Madrid. Tel. 34-91-372 91 70. Fax. 34-91-307 68 89) **Interlübke** (Gebrüder Lübke GmbH & Co.KG. Rheda -Wiedenbrück, 33378 Deutschland. Tel. 49-5242/12-1. Fax 49-5242/12-320); **Ivano Redaelli** (Via Brianza 4. 22040 **Lurago d'Erba** (Como) Italia. Tel. 39-031-607336. Fax 39-031-699185); **Jacadi** (Fortuny 51, 28020 Madrid, España Tel. 34-91-308 68 25. Fax 34-91-319 47 27); **Laura Ashley** (England); **Lema Spa** (22040 Alzate Brianza (Co) Italia. Tel. 39-031-63 09 90. Fax 39-031-63 24 92); **Liévore Asociados** (Plaça Berenguer, 1, Barcelona, España. Tel. 34-93-310 32 92. Fax 34-93-310 41 23); **Molteni & Co** (20034 Giussano (Milano), Italia. Tel. 39-0362-3591. Fax 39-0362-85 23 37); **Paola Lenti** (Via XX Settembre 7. 20036 Meda (MI) Italia. Tel. 39-0362-343216. Fax 39-0362-70492. E-mail: palenti@tin.it); **Poliform Spa** (Via Montesanto, 28, Inverigo (CO), Italia. Tel. 39-031-6951. Fax 39-031-699 444. www.poliform.it. E-mail: info.poliform@poliform.it); **Potterybarn** (Mail Order Department. P.O. Box 7044, San Francisco, CA 94120-7044 (USA); **The Iron Bed** (61184 Karben, Deutschland. Tel. 49-01805-214547. Fax 49-060 39-44 5 32); **Tisettanta** (20034 Giussano (Milano) Italia. Tel. 39-0362-3191. Fax 39-0362-31 93 00); **United Designers Limited** (37 Shad Thames Butlers Wharf, London SE1 2NJ. Tel. 44-171-3576006. Fax 44-171-357 8008).

PHOTOGRAPHERS

Santi Caleca (pages 55, 69, 70, 71, 92)
Cristina Fiorentini (page 80)
Mateo Piazza (pages 52, 77, 88, 91)
Margherita del Piano (page 75)
Jordi Sarrá (page 90)
Vega MG (pages 15, 30, 31, 50, 51, 62, 63, 75)